Poetic Memoirs

Warren Finn

Published in 2013 by FeedARead.com Publishing –
Arts Council funded

A CIP catalogue record for this title is available from
the British Library.

Ode to Medway

I used to walk the basin valley,
From Brompton Barracks to Ocelot's galley!

I used to wander with my daughters,
Around the defensive shield of Dockyard waters!

I used to watch the engineers run,
From the Army and Navy to the Setting Sun!

And I used to laugh with Ghurkhas of Nepal,
As we dined at Sun Pier to the signalman's call!

Now as memory conveys where once we stood,
Where men crafted Victory from walls of wood!

I remember jostled faces of re-conditions,
The submarines built on expanded positions!

I remember the rose of Upnor's fable,
When the Dutch arrived to turn the table!

I recall the waltz on Watling Street,
and Amherst echoes on Kitcheners seat!

I recall your knowledge of Fort Pitt stories,
About hospital heroes and medical glories!

I recall our chants for local teams,
The Livingstone Arms and liquid extremes!

And I still look for the rails of previous life.
As I walk the Dickensian footsteps with my wife.

And now as I let memory gaze beyond the marina sea,
Past changing skylines of housing and commercial property.

I can still extol virtues where skills gather dust,
And pay homage to those (who will listen) to your heritage past!

3

Navy Days (A Parody for Tennyson)

I rose at first light, ablaze with hope,
That shot sleeping harboured rope.
And reached my frigate travelled here,
To whistle waking mornings cheer!

And when murky sands tempted May,
From coves of history and wearied bay,
The regimented tricks began,
Enacting combat for fellow man!

My mother clung about my neck,
While father raved of death and wreck,
Upon silent shores now far from home,
Where phantom darkness no longer roam!

Childhood

Where do all the heroes go
when there's no one left to save?
Captain scarlet, where are you now,
won't you chase my blues away?
Joe 90 - I'm calling you:
Won't you come and save the day?
Because International Rescue
they can't come out to play!

Starting School

My first day in school, the greatest public affair,
Saw friends and family gathered, for one so unaware.
A most noble state occasion to help me on my way,
By goading and cajoling me towards the 'most ponderous' of days!

A few faces I recognised, although many I did not,
But later, like the others, I finally grasped the plot.
Big brother took me in hand and admonished all my fears
By saying 'he'd see me later' whilst gloating at my tears.

Whilst forlorn in the playground, a woman did make a noise.
Which children all assembled to and girls did sit with boys!
A new face came to greet us, who would take us all the year
I wondered if my parents knew how long I would be here?

She asked us many questions and plied us with her sums,
But if she didn't know the answers she should have asked our
Mums!
She tried to get our attention by asking what we all would be!
Would we aspire as nurses, or doctors, or sail a distant sea?

Well at this point, I realised then, that I was different from the rest.
I thought long and hard about my response. It would outdo the
very best!
So with my biggest breath - I shared what I would be.
When I grow up Miss - I'm going to be Paul McCartney!

Wordsworse Nonsense

I weighted lonely for chips and cod,
That floats on fat over oils and spills,
When all at once I saw something odd,
A host of money changed for Pils,
Beside the road, beneath the signs
Vomiting and brawling – passing lines

Counting sirens as the sirens shine
They stretched in never-ending grime,
Prostitutes plied their murky way
Along the high street of the day,
Five people saw I at a glance
All kicking heads in sprightly dance!

The Bill came and joined the song,
But Wayne forgot to sing along.
He out-did the swarming blues in glee,
And died in cheerful company,
A Poet gazed – but never thought
Or remarked on the fame their wealth had
brought.

For oft, when on your couch I lie,
In petty of defensive mood,
They dash upon my inward eye
Which is the pain of solitude,
And then my heart displeasure fills
And cries for Wordsworth daffodils!

How To Win Votes In The Political Arena

I took a walk through the city today.
Through rat-runs and shop fronts to while away.

I saw people gathered and walking through,
Burgeoning piles of doggy do.

I thought for a moment what could be done.
To rid the plight of scented dung!

Maybe Vicars could bewail the rising cost,
For a decline in takings and man-hours lost?

Maybe Councillors could beseech their political friends,
To ensconce four-legged loos on every bend!

Perhaps, inventors could conceive something more super,
Something more radical than the steaming scooper!

Maybe Leaders could challenge and despatch my name,
And applaud the triumph on bringing shame!

Or maybe they could sign a New Year's mention,
That would rid the world of excrement ascension!

And perhaps before mounting the word on the street,
They could assist with the oozing mass clinging to my feet!

What Constitutes Friendship?

I was once asked a question that went like this:
Can you describe friendship with a single kiss?

Pondering extensively – I put pen to paper
And made my response for you to decipher!

If you ask me the question – then friends we are not,
Because friendship is more than the names you've forgot!

Friendship is allowing your voice to be heard,
About taking direction – however absurd!

Friendship is more than the ring on your finger,
It's more than the menu on which you now linger!

It's more than the angels who declined a wing,
And it's more than the melody that makes everybody sing!

Friendship is about everything that we should always do,
To retain the alliance of someone like you!

The Problem With Geography

The Internet gave me access to questions from afar,
About influencing rainfall and eroding Zanzibar.
So when the teacher asked me about the deltas on the Nile
I typed a question to Jeeves and waited for a while.

But how was I too know that the Deltas were on tour?
Taking bookings in Burnley and the clubs of Cote de Jeure.
My teacher seemed quite peeved at stats on alcohol intake
Claiming my lack of piteous proof reading was just an
imbecilic mistake!

Modern Secrets

"Weren't you once a mod?" A friend once asked of you,
"Let's wipeout time for Glam rock crimes and the people
that we knew!"

With football chants still rising you soared upon the boards
Sailed away on vinyl streets - for the secrets that you scored.

Well Riley he's been harping for someone nearly there,
With Kris and Nine Below who shadowed in the glare.

With Modern Works still calling and plaudits by the score,
You trawled a distant journey along the Medway shore!

Childhood Imagination

The newspaper headline screamed the eggs had been killed:
They'd been found in a saucepan only partially filled.

Oats were formed and runny - scarred in the rooms
Hiding from Cheerio's and blood curdling spoons!

The Coco Pops awoke to a fiendish sight,
Of milk in the kitchen - left out through the night!

Cornflakes were tripping all over the sill,
While Weetabix was typing his last testament and will!

Fruit and Fibre shook their heads in disarray,
About the scene that befell them on that terrible day!

While strawberries and slices slued down the door,
Amongst the empty cartons now adorning the floor!

Through scattered yoghurt left alone in the sink,
The children awoke to a terrible stink!

"What's this I see?" voiced one daughter Krystal.
"I think mum's forgotten to wash – fore going to Bristol!"

"Shouldn't be allowed!" echoed Shanice from her bed,
"Perhaps the physician will look at her head!"

"It won't be no use!" Cried the BEKO chiller,
"Because this is the handiwork of a cereal killer!"

Chatham to Victoria

I never mislaid the love of travel,
I never misplaced the fear of standing too close,
Or the sense of urgency as carriages pulled out.

I still long for the aroma of diesel or steam,
I still long for the infectious world where I can gaze,
Or dream about lives racing by.

How I love the autonomy of the musical tracks,
The smooth rhythm of the engine tenor,
Gazing at replicated beauty in blackened windows!

How I long for the familiar prospect of guards,
the routine walk along light trodden platforms,
And the eventual decline into the underground.

I still smirk at the station you baptized after me,
And enlighten my children that 'I owe it all to you'
And now they entertain my ramblings supplying their
memories!

Daybreak

Slowly, but silently awake the gloom,
Alight the shadow and spin the moon,
Over mountains, hilltops, valleys and streams,
Shine silver light; upon silver beams.

Slowly but surely – the stars you'll catch
The waking man and the harvest thatch;
The curse of cars and lavender's sheets,
Among the steadfast, vaunted streets.

Across the plaited, patent door,
Across the ribbon, muse of before.
Your silver strands will pass us by,
As warm down shields; the sleeping eye!

Humpty's Last Stand

The crowds had gathered for the day,
To see if Humpty would run away,
The time had come for him to fall,
From the rose lined secrets of the garden wall.

The soldiers, they'd gathered in the park,
To join in the spectacle of yonder laugh,
The press they waited with baited breath,
As Humpty leapt towards his death.

He fell upon the stone laid ground,
And made a rather squelching sound.
The King cried loud, "Now scrape him quick…
Before he makes the people sick!"

And swift as light the infantry moved in,
And placed his contents in a bin.
"Hooray" they cheered, "he now looks thinner"
As they scrambled eggs for a celebratory dinner.

Well-known Celebrity Suicide

Humpty Dumpty stood up high,
Yet no longer waved at the adorning sky,
He saluted the cavalry that scarred the sound,
And chastised the cannons that littered the ground.

"How could they be so cruel to each other?"
"Soldiers in arms…. brother against brother!"
And as he wept torn tears and watched them fall,
He stepped silently from the awaiting wall.

And as the ground enveloped his departing life,
He wept for the waking of his mourning wife!
He wept for the brothers that would laugh no more,
And he wept for the sisters who sighed on the shore!

He wept for the shadows of departing days,
He wept for the sunrise silence of morning haze!
And he wept for the futility of his final act,
And for the closing solace created by that!

What if?

When Justin Wainwright arrived at school,
His face was shaped like a paddling pool!
All knobbles and scarred – from head to foot,
Eyes bright red, yet black as soot!

"He can sit down there – next to you!
You look the same – Your tops are blue!
He'll need a friend to help him learn,
So just keep quiet and wait your turn!"

Then teacher wrote upon the board.
Can you tell me about King Arthur's sword?
And in a flash – his hand waved in the air.
"Please Miss ask me, I was there!"

"How could you be? You stupid child.
A time of Knights; when life was wild!
A place of Kings, Barons and Earls.
When men were savages and boys were girls!"

Justin Wainwright left that day,
I hear he went on to write a play,
About Sorcerers, Kings and Barons eleven,
It became a movie – the kingdom of heaven!

The Theatre Royal (The Lady on the Hill)

Dear Lady, what treasures do you keep from my view?
What thoughts are you shrouding?
Can I share them too?
Where is the mystery that once you belied?
Is it just sleeping? Or has it just died?

For many years now, you've stood upon this shore.
A testament to a life lived long before.
And the excessive beauty that once you adorned,
Has paled with a time; that's now sadly mourned.

Your name, that's emblazoned for everyone to see;
Now taints the heart that beats within me.
For when the wind blows, where God's did reside.
I wonder: how safe are the secrets you hide?

Classroom Nonsense

"Taint fair," said Josh, "I don't get the pun!
How can Literacy be so much fun?"
"That's easy," said Jamie, with bright golden hair
"The girl of my dreams she sits over there!"

Well Daisy replied, "That's of little use
The comments you make are to obtuse!"
"That's easy for you" said Shane to his friend,
As he scooted his potty off round the bend.

While deep in the darkness the teacher stepped in,
"I don't know what your thinking" he grinned with a grin.
"Don't worry" said Daniel asleep in his bed,
"My brain is still reeling from the things that you've said!"

"I hope you're finished – we're nearly at break.
Have you proof read your work and changed the mistake?"
"Don't be crazy Sir" was the reply,
"Are you taking drugs?" a unified cry.

He wept aloud, "Please pander my whimsy,
Stop making your excuses evermore flimsy!
Try it today – it's not very hard;
Or be sold at Tesco's along with the lard!"

The Candy Box

There's fudge that comes in all shapes and sizes,
Candy coated liquorice and lemon surprises,
There's milk chocolate melts and ice cream wishes,
Banana splits a plenty; and apple pie kisses!

So before you make your way to the other part of town,
Try a soda pop harpsichord or a caramelised crown,
Try a sugar filled lemon or a vanilla fondant slice,
But please don't choke on the marshmallow splice!

A Picnic In The Park

While pitching fish at lilac skies,
I saw chocolate cakes go sailing by,
Penguin biscuits now grinned for me,
As half eaten sandwiches bounded out in glee.

And as swans gathered - to show their repose,
To contrast the slingshot where chocolate folly goes,
With swordfish grins we set out once again,
To skim currants and cutlery out after them!

Pharsipal Notense

"The harsh of mare", states the troubled shoe
"Shall reign today…before I flew"
And for shake all others, before the butler
To skin the Geronimo that crumble did Custer!

Well shiver me whimpers and fill me tenders
I fish the pentatonic…that Muriel senders.
So…grass the grace of tireless tunes
And ladle the liquorice of plantatoons.

"Plethora Pickle", well me thinks, "She tries….
Shall speckle idioms before sunrise…."
While Walkers run the goads of Rage….
Along the webbed corn balustrade!

So banquet bequeath the plighted poor
And sweep the girl who kissed the moor….
For; he will love before a day's repeat
And Risk the run of Tavia's treat!

Christmas Wishes

Diamond darting as morning lights,
While summer shares a cursive slight,
Before lapping tongues of foaming white,
Bury their teeth in briar trite.

Now as the still tides of mourning night,
Wake autumn glimpse of tired alms respite,
Before the throngs of deaf delight,
We whisper solace for those who fight.

Sons'…now marching on to war,
Repent the sins of those before,
Who in their turn lay shadows down?
Along farrowed fields of twisted crown!

So, when crimson grapeshot scars the morn,
Where weeping ghosts still feed the dawn,
I'll stand aloft…a last lament,
And remember names braised on grey cement!

Oh Brother!

I wish my brother he weren't so bright,
To send my balloon floating off through the night!
And I wish he wouldn't ask me to lead,
Before the nettles (that bite) have gone to seed!

Oh how does my brother think of these things?
The bumps on heads and the knees that now sting!
Surely, he wasn't always this clever
To allow me no choice in his personal endeavour!

Surely, there was once a time,
Before the lumps and bruises were only mine?
And where, oh where did he get the sense?
To tease and tie me to the garden fence!

A Gift From God?

We'd been expecting him for most of our years,
My father was happy, my mother in tears.

So when we awoke to follow from our bed,
We weren't quite prepared for the things that you said!

"A gift from God!" Did I hear right?
Because when I looked in there was a horrible sight!

There she slept with fiery, furnace, grin,
Not afraid of the smiles of those gawping in!

"So what happened to the boy, our new baby brother?"
I made this request from my now sleeping mother.

"Couldn't we send her back?" was brother's request?
With prose of Aston Martin's now vacating his chest!

Conaurd Burturn

On painted moor and shall-ed bray
On sullied morn and coppered hay
On twee lee horns and scal-ed brechts
They shimmied time which interjects

Long twa-la-brie and potted miles
Long casted glance that never styles
Long gravelled daze and Stella nights
Chester lost for wept delights

In sequined mires and resined streams
In coloured ash and milled extremes
In ghosts of born and acrid maize
A child forgot and turned to wave

On sullied mounts and sheltered folds
On heathered days with tales untold
On ventured brooks and plays of then
A just reminder extolled of when

Through Khepri dawns and boisterous brows
Through Anubis thoughts and Horus boughs
Through lacquered lawns and books of write
The piper danced his final light

Whilst others speak of 'morrow men'
Whilst Sabian looks and weeps again
Whilst Pontiffs reflect and then take flight
A day was lost to worldly slight?

A Falkland Friend

I remember waving from the dockyard wall,
Wishing you well as - I recall.
'Unfortunate' that someone was still back at home,
'Waiting for a call' on the telephone.

So take care 'Dear David' keep 'your head down low'
Let your 'officer guide you in all that you know'
We 'look forward to the party when you get back'
'Keep out of the way' if they should attack!

Reward

"No one should be rewarded – Tis not a noble deed!"
"For what I do – I do for you – that's all that I concede"

"As battle cries are over and drummers cease retreat
Don't gather on the hillside - to still the vacant seat!"

For on tangled grasses retiring - journeyed valours sight,
You'll miss the deed and all its greed – where summer's
used to light.

So be swift when raising glasses - sublime for those
without,
Now folly shades linger to scourge the battle route!

David

Now that I have gone to sleep,
I still reside, where you do weep,
For in the land, that I did roam,
There's still a place that I call home!

Lift up your hearts to all you see,
For what you see is part of me,
And when you wake to meet the day,
You'll find me where the children play!

For I am the wind, the sun and rain,
And the morning dew on ripened grain,
I am the moon that lights your night
Because I'm still here to guide your sight!

I am the dawn that brings the day,
And I am the sunlight that dry's the hay,
And I am the path that you wearily tread,
And I am the harvest that provides the bread!

So when you wake and try to see,
Do not despair when you think of me,
For I still hear you call my name,
Because I am the wind you try to tame!

So do not mourn and do not weep,
I have not left I only sleep,
For I am the dust beneath all feet,
And a brother to those I've yet to meet!

A View From The Battlements

We view where we lay in a summers haze,
Not daring to relocate from our turreted wall.
We watched while picnics began the pursuit
Safe in the knowledge they posed no peril!

With steeples still rising across infamy,
The treachery of time with spectres overthrown,
Still seek to encourage innovative trade,
And yet there are no arms to do battle!

The walls still unyielding and with archers' viewpoint,
Knew that the passing of time had shaped footholds,
Only pigeons now languished where man once tunnelled,
The Galleries now alive with the pursuit of a view!

For why should we fear the safety of battlements?
Placed many years before to allege the malevolent,
Placards now safeguard and sustain all life contained,
And occasionally shield against the enemy!

The Man of Kent

You used to live in Rochester – that's what I heard you say.
Was it by the Tideway, or the Charm of Mandolay?
Was it by St. Margaret's that Castle's in the night?
Or was it by St. John's - where the locals like to fight?

Tales from the Tributary

Glimmering and immeasurable absent from tranquil slues,
The window of sweet night air is now still and blanched.
Save for the residue of line spray and ponies stilled hooves,
Listen and hear the final call of ships now ranched!

And with turbid tides flowing back through the estuary,
The wind will continue to tussle over the darkening plain.
Gillingham will whisper for the cost of human misery,
In melancholies extensive, withdrawing exclaim!

The maritime dance, steps tranquil tonight,
now the surge is complete and the mood libel fair.
Upon the strait on St. Mary's beach perceive the light,
that glistens, consumes, where cranes overhang sleeping stare!

Midnight waves now play shingle, which snags and then is flung;
shall we wait for their return up high on the strand?
At the ebb of the tide where stories cease and begun,
the eternal echo of cadence will bring sorrow to the hand!

The Nags

Angie still serving trannies and queers,
But the greeting you'll get there is always sincere!

Jim's at the bar now - getting them in,
While Mandy's contented - drinking her gin!

And bands now play - where cues gather grime,
While local artists still collect - to analyse time!

Lost Innocence

The London that I came to greet
Did once behold a Monarch's seat
But in the city of palace and tower
There now resides a deadly power.

Where are the noble that once did claim?
To be exacting of you fame.
Where is the innocence that once adorned?
Your hallowed paths before all was mourned.

Where was the band? Have they now played?
With dying soldiers and horses splayed.
Did time forget to simply measure?
And rob us all with cheap displeasure.

Where once past glories did reside,
A foreign wealth now swells the pride.
And ever busy will labours ply,
To grasp the power from native sky!

The multitude will swarm the wearied glow,
To catch the glimpse which you bestow,
And on such journeys will splendour hide,
The questions gleamed from ashen tide!

Ascended from such nobles eyes,
Will past indulgence ever surprise?
Will learned seek from all you hail?
Or simply gaze beneath the veil?

Now that we can see the cost,
Will we now mourn for all that's lost?
Will we remember the unsettling truth?
That was part of innoxious youth.

Or will we shelter in honoured shade,
Where our past glory did once parade?
Or will we let all charity shine,
For a city blooded by the un-divine?

Vain Glory

I'm sure to go to heaven –
because I've served my time in hell,
I've got nothing left to brag about –
I've got nothing left to tell.

Don't waste my time with futile crime –
don't tell me that I'm wrong,
Cos I know where I'm going to –
and that's where you don't belong!

You stand around with vacant frown –
you're begging to hang on,
But what you never realised then –
is your day has been and gone!

A half-crazed mind on overtime –
trying to be the clown,
Verbal contracts taken out –
but know one to write them down!

Well you're sure to go to heaven –
cos you've made my life pure hell,
With you illustrious acceptance that tirelessly befell!

29

Chanting From the Terraces

The echoes of obsession now enters semblance view,
As Cody McDonald positions and enters the ring,
While Linganzi bows with Matt Fish too,
Boardroom brigades coerce Weston to step in,
Exhilaration rises and limbers referred ranks,
Will Kedwell play to revoke previous partiality?
As Martin and Wheldale present and sweep thanks!
Now Adebayo beams to tepid faces of obscurity!

A tribal stance now cranking Davies passion,
Allen center fakes and fades to the right,
Among seas of blue now sporting their fashion,
When Bradley surges as Leon alights,
Gloating gossip now somewhat cowed,
To receive downfield a waiting boot.
Among wallowing whispers that once rang loud.
Nelson now postures and begins to shoot!

Red Card

"So your off to watch the final and see them lose again!
Weren't you punished enough last time when going
down to ten?"
"Will this be every Saturday? Will you be back for tea?
Will this be my life forever? A widow of stripped blue
sea!"
"Well don't expect to find me waiting - to red card in
the hall.
And the kitchen's now off limits - since the red carding
on the wall."
And the lounge is now for telly - where red cards used
to lie.
So just remember that - when the goals go flying by!"

Depressive Of The World Unite

If I reveal not now the cause
With stunted breath and stilted pause
I could forsake my life this day
On hallowed time with sweet array
If I bare witness to the cost
Where once you stood, before all was lost
I could forsake my life this day
And see the truth with sweet array
If I reveal the guilty life
To caring husband and doting wife
I would bear witness to the pain
That life no more in thee would reign.

Part II

So sadness cast your shadow deep,
No night to scorn, No dawn to weep.
Take us to your unloved place,
Where we may see our fall from grace!
Let you shadows sweep away,
An ungrateful voice – in a life filled day,
Let us learn by our mistakes,
To rejoice in knowing what life takes.
Be patient, so that we may learn,
To enjoy our life and enjoy our turn!

Is Destiny Ours?

Look closely and you will see
Infinite wisdom I give to thee?
For if you do not take a chance
Expect for nothing that will enhance.

Such aspirations are plain to me
Avert your eyes and you will see!
But don't look close when it's made clear
In case you mistake me for insincere.

Take your time, now is this true?
Callous message, is it for you?
Hurtful perhaps – could this be fact?
Ask another - how does he react?

Next time don't be so bold,
Discern it first and then take hold!
Take your time – well could it be true?
Hasteful remarks, will debate all anew!

Extra time is what you require,
Not everyone gets what they desire?
You will need to take a second look,
Only to help with what you mistook.

Underlying message – it's all quite plain
Daylight of knowledge – will eventually reign.
In case you have overlooked the clue,
Eclipse the ones that are not for you!

Such is the message standing bold,
Hasten your quest - let it take hold.
Infinite clues I've given to thee,
Times running out – will you but see?

Hasten your vision – can you see what I say?
Expect the unexpected – not simple display
As we draw near – I'll try to amend
Despair is not the means to an end!

A Musical Tale

Whilst en route for hurrying ranks - beside the melody mile,
Vibes of Hart protracted from tempo backbeat style.
And as the pitch grew narrow – we faded from within,
Along rapidly changing tempos towards Zematis sting!

And by preserving lunchtime steadfast - with lazy drinking day
Kris thought to fly the crowds and fulfil in his dismay,
As ambience surged and resonated – all the phoney's gone,
The hope of decorated grandeur spurred the sundry on!

I waltzed through East End memoirs and sang along too many;
Let my imagination wander through sidelined intentioned Rennie,
There were riffs of plague objectives and beliefs of Southern Belle
Shows at Detling fairgrounds and angels posing well!

But as the piper's music fiddled and scourged the baited ground,
You jibbed at unknown tourists visiting all around,
So when painted mural faces echoed foremost wall,
Foggy spectred references cried towards the whispered hall!

Leftfield Limericks

Leftfield Limericks should they be clever?
Should they ruse the carnival and go on forever?
Should they recant tales of nights spent in Paris?
Or make malicious demands of Anita Harris?
Should they reminisce for previous affection?
Or dedicate a sonnet to a passing reflection?

The Spirit of My Heart (The Country Song)

I've been drifting through the country - so make no mistake,
For the fortune I'm now seeing - standing by the lake.
When the angels of my winter - no longer pass me by
I'll beg for some repose - from the spirit of the sky.

Well I can't help wondering - what brought me next to you,
While the serpents of their tongues - pierce my body through
As the days grow warmer - you'll hear me from the crowd
I'm still dreaming out of place – dreaming out loud.

I've been visualising you - before we ever met
I've been visualising you - so much - I won't regret,
If the devil comes and takes me - before I touch your hand,
The spirit of my heart - will always understand.

So pardon me please – as I slowly pass you by,
But the beauty I'm now seeing - makes me want to cry,
The way you step in motion - wakes a sleeping heart,
As the essence of your beauty - tears my soul apart!

And should I hear your whisper – calling out to me
I'll be speaking with the preacher - standing next to me
I'll be listening to the words - that placed upon my hand,
The spirit of my heart that - we all understand!

I've been drifting through the country - so make no mistake,
For the fortune I'm now seeing - standing by the lake.
When the angels of my winter - no longer pass me by
I'll beg for some repose - from the spirit of the sky.

The Voice of Summer

I heard Miss Summer Calling;
She crept slowly from her home,
And rubbed her sleeping eyes;
And cleansed the sweeping gnome!

She breathed warmth at every window;
And life to every door,
And presents the trees with waking leaves,
That winter cast upon the floor.

Her breath awakened every puddle;
That winter thought was his,
And dispelled the morning mist;
Before fauna stemmed what is!

She waved her arms at darkness;
As people hid the coal:
From dusting days of winter,
That clung from pole to pole.

"Oh how we are warmed", was her whisper;
That warned my waking way'
As I sailed a golden journey,
Across a summer's day!

In My Life (A note for John)

There are places – that are not to be!

All my life cursed winters still arrive for me,

Some forever voiced discussions raise remnants glories,

While some have gone to report closing stories!

And these places still field images of condemnation,

With lovers and friends of a lost generation,

Some still adorning photos of fresh-faced youth,

In my life - I've loved always those followers of truth!

The Collector

Weariness woke this morning;
Dressed in shards of grey!
And took away the sunshine,
That filled the breaking day.

The turning of the hands,
They tolled the turning time,
And brought forth an audience,
To await - the passing chime.

Hushed tones of mourners;
Filed past to greet your son.
And spread melodic malady;
On each and everyone.

No smiles to comfort memories.
No touch to free the pain;
Just silent, reflected monotony
That tides could not contain!

The strumming of the rain clouds,
Etched within each thought,
And filled the cloistered monograph,
Of each deliberated report.

Innocent tears of children,
Dutifully wept on stairs,
While final folding curtains,
Awoke the waiting stares!

A collector called this morning,
He didn't leave his name.
But he left us all in silence,
Will life – ever be the same?

The Last Hussar

How will you remember me? When I am gone?
When there's no more to see!
Will your thoughts stray? Or parody?
In unlikely remembrance of me!

When you can no more see me,
or revel in my pallid light,
Who will you turn to in haste?
To gain your paltry sight!

Well Pappus beings I say to thee;
Your Gloss will sheen no more!
Because my future runs different now,
to the objectives you vainly restore.

A cornerstone I may not be?
But tread wearily around corollary remarks,
For who will you turn to, when I am no more,
to gain your failing laughs?

Wise men have tried to better me?
Whilst fools have shown the way!
I've watched them all in turn enact,
their pantomime unleavened display.

Better by far you should forget and smile
and foment your own desire
Because if you wanted my opinion,
then you would only be a liar!

Don't tell me of your future plans
because for me I have no part
Because tomorrow I inert halcyon Glory,
bereft of languid heart

So extravasate your just concerns
and prepare your guileless wits?
Because that's all that I have come to expect,
from a bunch of useless gits!

Eveline

For what reason did I betray my liberty?
Was I so fickle to accept a smile and; therefore seal my fate?
Or did I realize the call of destiny?
Did I accept it readily? For an answer – I'll wait!
You walked into life and distilled all cause
Did I accept your burning desire or calming ideal?
Growing ever more patient never bowing to applause
Were you imagined? Or accepted for real?
Did virtues awake; that had since lay dormant?
Leaving all before you. Beauty I craved!
Did despair set in at the power you could cement?
Accepting control of heart, so readily enslaved
What was the reason for acceptance of tyranny?
With your calming thoughts and the gentleness of a dove
Why did I relinquish my heartfelt liberty?
I relinquished everything to gain all, LOVE!

The Last Farewell

If you could see the pain I grieve,
For loves lost cause on summers eve,
And if by chance, you glance my face,
A shattered smile; now takes its place.
Five long years to live a lie,
With broken heart, no tears to cry,
Dusting dreams to sweep away,
A long lost cause; a remembered day.
Take a bow and leave the stage,
See the book for a better page.
Until such time; all things are past,
A love like this could never last!

A Man Of Honour?

Whilst thinking of careers – I searched for some redress,
From victims I did chastise – and thoughts they did express,
By ignoring their well-being – and scoffing at a dream,
I carved a worthwhile life – for a man of little esteem!

A Man of Fame?

Well – I've flirted with fortune and wandered through fame,
With a reputation intact – and a knighthood to claim,
Is my life therefore worthy of an extravagant story?
Or merely a cardboard response to an unnerved glory?

A Man of Fortune?

'Throw caution to the wind' – a man once said to me,
In spite of this consideration – I forgot my usual tenacity,
Whilst recoiling in my thoughts – to plan the perfect crime,
I met a nice policeman – who helped me with a fine!

Nobody's Hero

Your cultured view expresses nothing but banal reality!
And your whimsical tone highlights your own frailty!
So don't be clever – and attempt to articulate your thought,
Because your views are repressed and your knowledge is
fraught!

Because within the field of innovative displeasure,
I STOLE THE FINAL GLANCE FROM ALL THAT YOU
TREASURE!
And when the dead woke – to claim yet another day,
Aristotle bought the last train ticket and got lost in the fray!

The Gallery

In placid hours unbridled scheme,
On pictorial waters that touch serene,
Where energies begin and then create,
A moment's reflection for the Tate.

Should lovers swim or smile the freeze?
While patience stills the beckoning breeze?
Will humility scorn and then take pride,
For revered reflections that try to hide?

The Unseen Kingdom

As I wandered down Chancery Lane,
I thought I heard you call my name,
'Pass the old man at the paper stand'
Was where I could disappear to another land!

So I descended down to your beckoning call,
And surveyed the kingdom that seduced your wall,
And when I saw the lines – that were still as yet unseen
I grasped for the money to covet your theme.

I took my place for the price of a day,
And slide down even further to where courts held sway,
And with your loyal subjects – we could only but fain,
To journey still further as we mounted the train!

Your kingdom began to unfold before my eyes,
As I journeyed through Kilburn to see Kensal Rise,
As I travelled from Blackfriars to where Earls held Court,
I wondered if St. James was happy with the Park that he
bought!

Tower Hill was more than the name it addressed,
And the Monument was less than the view it expressed,
And Mansion House could still - be seen from afar,
So long as you had the time to travel by car!

And still the names were lost upon my sight,
As Charing Cross altered and changed the route of my flight,
And with undivided remorse I snuck out once again,
To be chastised by a city awashed in rain!

And as I gazed beneath the darkened sky's,
A final reminder embraced my eyes,
With neon lights showing the way - for all to see,
I caught the last show at the Circus of Piccadilly!

The New Dawn

Cast out the demons; Cast out the lies,
Cast out the untruth which beauty denies,
Cast out the ghost; that time has now past,
Embrace now with a heart; a love to last.

Search for a life; Search for a love,
Search for somebody who shares your love.
Search for the magic; that ignites so much,
And you'll find true love in all that you touch!

And as life wakes you to another dawn,
You'll touch the face where love is born,
And in the beauty of waking eyes,
You'll smile and laugh at the impending skies!

A Taste of Two Cities

I once knew a Brassiere steeped in Bengal,
Whose dishes were treasured from Rochester to Nepal?
Whose mangoes were famous for pickling fresh chutney?
From platforms of Chatham to the Half Moon at Putney!

The Origins of Ruby

She came from Mesopotamia sailed an Indian dawn,
A blend of scented spices on weathered turmeric storm,
Where Masala ginger etched Easter bonnet laws,
On chillier, marinated delicacies that conducted world
applause!

She soothed Biryani basted chickens and Korma crested
crowns,
Rice of plain and pillau and phalli platted gowns,
She lingered on my taste buds and kept her secret near,
While Cobra coated moments raised a glass in cheer!

Rochester by Moonlight

In former streets of splendour where Satire songs applied,
I'll walk forever in serenity where restoration now resides!

While gangs replete in carnage will gawp your silent lanes,
Chronicled tones of narration will chase childish refrain!

And as the chill of romance fuels moonlit avenues bliss,
I'll compose these vines of poetry left by Cathedral's kiss!

The Girl from McDonald's

You used to sneer at waiting concerts and surf the
gathering crowds,
Where Milkshake men and Prisoners kept sixties beat
aloud.

Always a welcoming comment - keeping my cholesterol
high,
With flirtatious overtones still trying to catch my eye,

And when discussing all before you – with alluring eyes
receding,
Dentistry diagraphs commenced forthwith - to begin
ballroom proceedings!

But the time was never conducive to join me or
compare,
So I sought solace in your smile as I viewed you from over
there!

Creatures of the Night
What's the creature that rattles the roof?
That scoffs at the sunset and stands quite aloof?
What's the creature who scorns window panes?
Who scatters the leaves and drives them insane?
What's the creature who slaps shutters tight?
Whenever the storm rages out through the night.
And what's the creature who pales with a shrill,
With the power to bring life, damage or kill?

The Final Waltz

A silent smile encompassing her lips,
Construct me true my worthy master!
Score round the bows of departing ships,
That shall forever laugh at future disaster,
As the swirl and depression of the ride,
Shall wave with whirlwind and finally wrestle,
That once stood steadily at anchors tide,
Shall remember where once they built your finest vessel.

So tower the vast Victory and stand her tall,
With cannon decks raised and courage in the air,
Where pictures adorn books and office wall,
Cast out your final prayers for the men waiting there,
Now signal the lanterns and release the moat,
As ships companies welcome another to the crown,
Stand near on the drawbridge and let her life float,
Glimpse the spectres of prayers still looking down!

A craft as cordiality in history stanch,
With once a voice that complete of beamed glee,
Shall no longer wait for the message: "Shall we launch?"
Or weather the wintered tide of oceaned sea!
And what shall become of the replica the Master brought?
That crafted the finest galleys with refined skills of art,
Where is the greatest labour now that might be wrought?
Once perfected and planed in every part!

An Unexpected Arrival

Through tears of emotions with three lives at risk,
Life was given. Frail and premature yet battling to hang on!

Weighing less than anything fully formed
– too small to survive,
Only the prayers of those would eventually provide an
answer!

How much longer will you be able to swim?
As minutes pass like hours against the deluge of tides,
Will the voice of reason ever penetrate expectancy?
And will you have the strength to retain life?

Will the exhaustion of your struggle engulf you?
Will your wounded essence ever repair?
Will your need of strength ever surge to give being?
Or will threads of vulnerability be lost in a maritime of pain?

Footnote

To avoid the mistakes of youth?
Draw from the wisdom of age?

The only things we really lose
Are the things we try to keep?
The only things we cannot grasp,
Are the stars beyond our reach?
The only reason for listening today,
Is that tomorrow my never come!

WHATEVER HAPPENED TO THE BLANK GENERATION?

Dismiss all styles of plateresque, look closely beneath the
veneer,
Since uninspired judgement is always regarded sincere.
Lest caustic tongues draw anarchy from those that we detest,
Forget your unsung heroes and do what you do best.

If problems you desire, then problems there will be,
For if you do not question, then answer's you will see.

Decorticate all worthless shells forsake disparaging remarks
For insufficient reminders will only make us laugh.

Time's an apt reminder of all that we held dear
Delate with universal reasoning to notice all visions clear.

Forget hermetic reasoning break forth and start anew
Purport unknown desires and influence unalterable view.

Lest ignorance besets you, less intolerance makes you deride
Remember a time of cluttered desires, where once we all
arrived.

In casuist dreams we would follow and catalyse recognized
decrees
And forget what went before and strive to reach our needs.

Distempered youth of yesteryear shout forth your failing call
And decry all unbelievers and watch their shadows fall.

Forget the blank generation that overlooked our youth,
Because history is always kind to those that steal our truth!

September Song (The Origin of Renewal)

Darkness came – but night never shone upon a fated portrait of broken repose. Instead distorted angels by dissipated aggression leapt unprepared towards bogus exposition.

Those who had loved – would love no more! Now that everything lay fluid on the periphery of being. Lifeless unease – forever broken by a September Song - which will forever encompass.

The forlorn scratched the surface of evident chaos, while others escaped the media glare entrenched in ruin. Picking through a labyrinth of debris that refused to give up its secret from abhorrent spectres of indifference.

The non-essential uneasily settled where once they were. Eyes filled with acrimonious woe! Eternally hunting the still tide of ash. Still hoping that the slay of friends would emerge from where they ceased!

And still the camera rolled, captivated by horror and disbelief, as you toppled to complete the descent. No hand to catch you – now shunned by sorrow – drowning in a remorseless vestige of remembrance.

What lies are you burning now? What stories have died – untold on your decaying floor? What sorrows can we ever drown to answer the waking screams of infants who are now orphaned? Extinguished now – by an existence of tears!

The Second

Who saw the petal slip softly from the rose?
Who saw the sunset break on the calming sea?
Who saw the sunrise flash silently on the break?
Who saw the nightingale kissed by the shore?

Who saw the wave caught on the mend?
Who saw the child emit mist on the deck?
Who saw the coloured top spin silently from the hat?
And who saw the look that touched the time?

"I did," cried the voice from deep within,
"I saw it all uncluttered from sin!"
"I saw the beauty that life had to share,
Because I was the moment left in solitude there!"

Critics

It is easier to criticize than actually achieve!
But to write any other way, is to go against all I believe
For to print lies, where the truth has to be told,
Is to accept false coinage, instead of pure gold?
Reactionary divisions will implode a tainted tongue,
And impugne the disposition, that ordinate's the young!
Is it therefore easier to satisfy, by attempting to digress?
Or will messages duly diminish when related by the press?

Beacon of the Vanquished

I could scuttle the four-minute mile,
Wax lyrical over Hendrix or Voodoo Chile,
Write scripts for Hollywood or merely compose;
Events of obligation in my crack filled nose!

I could squander derisory remarks,
Give back the Holy Grail I stole for a laugh,
Hunt down villains with rattan canes,
Or convey revolution near Tolstoy's claims.

I could be fond of the women you crave;
Hide in the crowd and be ever so brave,
Turn jest into money with unending appeal,
Or still the ocean for the cost of a meal.

I could be this and so much less.
I could turn cartwheels in a red rubber dress;
Give life to those that have come to expect;
Or hide like always and avoid the regret?

Personification

When winds bring sleeping trees to dance,
In scurried chills aid steeped advance,
Their cold facade will watch no more,
As silent whispers echo the departing door,.
So moated castles can never protect,
The decaying shorelines of your regret,
And when winter calls to advance the spring,
The sweeping clouds will change everything!

Sometimes

How can we not be stirred by concern; to sever the path of injustice?
How can we endorse rights; by never challenging the guilty?
And how can we stand by; and trivialise the plight of mankind, when we ourselves are never prepared to hinder the flood of intolerance?

Sometimes; it falls to one generation to break boundaries!
To drive a wedge through frontiers of accepted insensibilities.
Sometimes; it falls to one generation to go beyond fortunes distance!
To move mountains; with their rhetoric of insistence!

How can we call ourselves humane?
When through our own exception; we never bring inequality to account?
How can we accuse others; when we lack the moral courage to stave
Inhumanities tide of accepted bigotry and discrimination?

Sometimes; it falls to one generation to combine and connect!
To ennoble their brother; and still tears of regret.
Sometimes; it falls to one generation to unite in compassion!
To move faceless leaders; to unify in common fashion.

Are we that generation?
Are we prepared to bring together the wealth of perseverance that will
Lead each person towards the Promised Land?
Are we the generation who will be remembered as having the courage to
Stave the mantle of inability; and thankless expression?

Sometimes; it falls to one generation to be great!
To show the hand; that forever transforms fate.
Sometimes; it falls to one generation to go beyond mere responsibility!
To incite the world; and purge the mental barriers of abject poverty.

Are we the nation who; along with our brothers and sisters, will take up the cross and amend inherent expectation?
Sometimes; all it requires is a single step and others will follow!

ARE YOU THAT PERSON?

Drowning In Irony

I will always triumph!
I will take another breath and continue from where I
left.
And when my heart dies and I continue to live,
Maybe, you will see me (one day) in all my wonder.
For I am like none you have ever known!

I will look soaring and toward the firmament,
And when the world around me shallows,
shining like the oceanic gleam from the diminishing
light,
I will watch ahead and secure my eyes.

I will breathe victory and resume where I left.
And when my heart dies and I inhabit,
Maybe, you will see me in my entire marvel?
I am like none you've ever known!

Like a kingdom slowly drowning in the sands of time,
I am a creation of your baseless loathing;
I am the odium you feign in the stars above.
Forever lost to your silhouette of greater things!

The Boy from Troy

Jimmy Elliot of Peter's Street,
Told wartime memoirs - I'm yet to repeat.
With tales of woe and Odeon reels,
One day I'll publish - for the boy in Deal!

The Proud and the Beautiful

The passing of time; never relinquishes the simple act
of love,
And although the years have turned faster than my
mind would like to admit,
Still, I gaze upon the beauty that will forever be mine!

Because; whilst I no longer reside upon your emerald
shore,
My life will never be stilled by the parting of a tide!
Since distance can never dull a judgement; endorsed by
Captains and Kings,
It can only but wait to run its final course.

So, as I recoil in my thoughts; I am reminded of your
unspoiled beauty,
And I recall the first time; I truly witnessed the fullness
of nature's folly; eclipsed by morning dew,
Enshrined by the subtle frame of peat stained hills.

And with every step I take; the ghost's of past re-enact
my journeyed memory,
And with every breath I breathe; I remember; and taste
the beauty of many;
Who will forever be witness to your name?

For where else could the simple act of a meal be turned
into a moment in history?
Where else could the simplicity of wine remain never to
be bettered?
And where else could a sun end; except into the
coolness of the sea; to end a perfect day?

Because every time I recount the regal air;
Or recall the stars that have played upon your screen,
Unrepentant emotion embraces my eyes with tears,
And remind me of the wonder of life!

And through such selfless action; I raise a glass to the
God's,
Safe in the knowledge that the cream of the country;
Has been baptized by the fairest of city's

Because, whilst many have tried to determine your
course;
And have eventually fallen under your enduring spell,
I have accepted that this is my time! And that this is my
life!
And I have realized that you are my Ireland!

A Favour To A Poet

Stop all the cars and park your decision,
Because my key no longer sparks the ignition,
Muffle the engine and empty the boot:
Bring out the magazines and the cold morning suit.

Let signals remain forever on red,
Spreading the message 'the Nova is dead'
Place lifting straps around her body with love,
While traffic policemen shred; their black cotton gloves.

She drove me North to South to East and West,
She took me away for a week of rest.
I thought she would be my everlasting song,
However, she's knackered – so I was wrong.

The motorways are not wanted; put out ribboned cones
Empty the ashtrays and remnants of scone.
Pour away the screen wash and summon the guard,
For her last post is now playing at the re-cycling yard.

Embarrassing Parents

My wife and children think I've lost the plot,
For forgetting birthdays and that what is not!
For liking marmite and cold tin beans,
And flaunting my liking for these cardinal scenes!

Good Morning St. Peter What Can I Do For You?

If I had my life to live would I do it just the same?
Let me ponder that a minute please before you judge again.
I was a man of noble race, but placed in lowly birth
Although fully understanding why I was here upon this earth

Now school days were the beginning of my long road to ruin
Since I only ever achieved, the most prominent mis-doing.
I bathed in approved disdain, from pedagogic slight
And excelled pedantic motion whilst watching all take flight.

Well here I did reside, too reach my lawful rights
Ever tireless in my quest to gain my just delights.
Although many tried tempting they couldn't change minds
To follow my path to praise and the riches I would find.

Well careers and houses came placing money in my life
And whilst mixing in new circles I met my cheating wife.
Undaunted by this task, I broke out to start anew
And that's where burdens began as they brought me here to
you!

Now in answer to the question I've reached utmost heights,
Surrounded by the Plebeians, amongst unworthy sights,
Whilst correcting worldly morals I've fought oxalic ideas
And heard repented splendour stained with graceless tears.

I speak the truth (not fully) but as much as I do dare
With personal law court judgements, rather than elsewhere,
My actions are therefore guarded and formed by what I am,
So what you see before you then is a potential superman!

Question

Now that my soul has been troubled by worldly lustre!
Can vanity restore what temptation did muster?
Wherein my body, my emotions are perplexed!
Can faith alone restore – a spirit so vexed?

Of conceited attacks that descend like rain!
Will the flesh yield with perpetual disdain?
Will my senses overcome? Or will darkness prevail?
Will God be my saviour – or will his Grace fail?

Can I really follow his unquestionable belief?
Can I to be a Christian and turn a new leaf?
Shall mercy reign, where all have calmed worldly assault?
Or will hell deride and obtain all through misguided fault?

Therefore, will I be judged on my remarks of intent?
Or will I bequeath the penance that I have now spent?
And in so doing, will I gain remission for all that I am,
Or will I simply be judged accordingly for being a man?

Sunday

Weariness ventured slowly down the street,
To absorb all proceedings with contrasted conceit,
Engulfing the spirit from the previous day,
By swallowing all signs of spirited display!
It's mood reflected the change in our sight,
By unifying the world in sterilised plight!

Doctor Feelgood

Late last night I got to thinking,
What would happen if I stopped drinking?
Would surgery prescribe me purple pills?
That whence consumed would make us ill.

By eight o'clock would we turn threads,
With pulsating rhythms traversing heads?
Or would we breach the Kent line coast,
And find ourselves dining on Canvey toast?

I used to be a Satellite?

I used to be a satellite who fanned the waiting smile,
Stole pleasured chords of Memphis along the Camden mile,
But now neon signs diminish amongst steel littered streets,
Where younger unnamed gather to facebook my repeat!

Uncle Johnny

Johnny caught an allergy that no one could explain,
It made him verbalise posterity to help relieve the pain.

He'd salivate and slobber with ever pretentious squeal,
While barking forth his orders to garner Royal appeal.

So thank you uncle Johnny and ensue discordant bluster,
It called us once to arms and helped our parents fluster!

It gripped a moments pleasure and steered us from the cold,
And gave voice to adolescence and memories for the old.

A Daily Prayer

God grant me grace in the prayers I say,
Grant me peace throughout my day:
And watch over me as I walk avenues of strife
And grant me peace to shine in life.
Preserve the memory of those we hold dear,
And watch over them all in the coming year;
And may we convey with grateful heart,
The spirit of adoration that you impart.
And to all parents bestow hope and joy,
In all the thoughts they've yet to deploy.
And preserve all brothers and sister too,
And may we return their reverence due?

Silliness Parodied

I am the captain of my fate
And the master of my soul,
I am the rhythm to the blues
And the rock upon the roll.
I am the horror of the shade
And the wrath upon the tears,
I am the forgotten voice
And the menace of the years.
I am the clutching silence
That bludgeons from the crowd,
I am the waking recollection
That one can never shroud.
I am the bloodied head
That's yet to be unbowed.
For I am the sleeping giant
That's yet to shout aloud!

Keeping Connected

I have many friends on the Internet (most, I've never met)
And yet everyday they hassle me to share my life regret!
They tell me what they like though - on unsolicited sea,
And yet, what they share - never appears to interest me!
So I request them ever so kindly - to go and get a life,
While I enjoy the intimacy with the beauty of my wife!

The Diary Of An Alcoholic

She was the gentlest of graceful things,
The calming beauty to my daylight wings,
She was the sweetest blossom to my summer retreat,
And the soft carpet slippers that warmed my feet.
Her simple dress enticed my era of rage,
And pleased my heart with sinuous stage.
And when she no longer sustained auxiliary mist,
I directed her magnificence for a moment like this!

Krystal's Question to Edward

When did the owl and the pussycat go to sea
in a beautiful pea green boat?
How did they take honey and lots of money
all wrapped in a five pound note?
And why did the owl gaze at the moon
while strumming a small guitar?
Couldn't they have just taken a taxi
or journeyed there in a car?

Limericks Bright And Dreary

There once was a girl in the choir,
Whose voice rose higher and higher,
She sang to the Gods,
While some dreary sods,
Did steal the lead from the Spire!

Now Jim was ever so jolly,
He would spend his life counting lolly,
One day for a laugh,
He bought a giraffe,
Now his world is a nonsensical folly!

There once was a girl who said "YES"
Who the boys did like to undress.
One day in alarm,
She showed off her charm,
And the rest you can probably guess!

The once was a boy Matthew Brian,
Whose past time was frequently lying.
He said he could swim,
While others plunged in,
Now his mother is constantly crying!

I once knew a boy from the Clyde,
Whose stomach was pickled inside,
He liked to eat sickles,
All rusty with pickles,
And that's why he probably died!

Limericks Bright And Dreary

Alone in the Forest of Dean,
I showed girls what they'd never seen,
While flashing my ass,
To the gathering class,
I was arrested for being obscene!

"My ambition" said one Daniel Boone,
"Is too teach everyone a new tune!"
But the lacking attention,
To the previous mention,
Left him lonely till June!

In Norway I met an old Viking,
Whose travels were rather exciting,
He'd cheat and he'd pillage,
Most every village,
But plunder was not to his liking!

A girl from Harrow called Janet,
Liked burying husbands in granite,
When asked to explain,
She did it again,
So eventually they moved her to Thanet!

I once knew a girl from Kilkenny,
Who liked to give kisses too many,
She'd wave to the crowd,
All terribly proud,
But prayers there never where any!

Childish Rhymes

Claimed a linguist from Brazil,
The nuts I have will make you ill,
Don't ever share at any function,
Or repeat the message at your compunction!

Harry Hussein from Argentina,
Came to Britain to speak after dinner,
Played to the crowds without any shame,
Now everyone appears to gawp at his name!

If I were a hangman would I pull the cord?
Would I stand before headlines to receive the applaud?
Would I delight in notoriety, or sit in the pew?
Or question myself for the evil you do?

Should one enterprise for lost institutions
For public probate without careful conclusions?
Should impostors impose for what they evade?
When incandesant accounts are carelessly made?

Whatever happened to the Corolla Clown?
With his painted on smile that circled the town?
Whatever happened to the oversized shoe?
The bright draped frippery of those that he knew?

And where are the balloons that lost every ruse?
From the Delaware flatlands to Ballantine cruise?
And where, oh where do they hide all the shrieks?
That haunted the children for weeks upon weeks?

Ode to Stupidity

We wear the myriad mask that lies,
That fabricates truth and shades our eyes,
With courting tears and heartfelt sighs,
We'll coax the weak and fan their cries!

And when in debt the human chide,
Will forget the vows to the weeping bride,
And subtleties will placate that extra mile,
As we mask humanity with our guile!

You Choose

We wear the myriad mask that lies,
As we disguise humanity with our guile!

With courting tears and heartfelt sighs,
No subtleties will placate that further mile!

We'll coax the weak and fan their cries,
That forgot the vows to the weeping bride!

And fabricating veracity that tints our eyes,
We'll allow the debt of human chide!

Does Poetry Have To Rhyme?

Does poetry have to rhyme? NO!
Does it have to have meaning? Only to those who enjoy it!
Does it have to make sense? Only to avoid being nonsense!
Should it be so much more? Only if you want it to be!

The End of Our Year

What happens to all the stories when the gates are finally
closed?
Where will chants of playtime go when teachers wave their
farewell on the next stage of our lives?
And where do goalmouth stands reside when fields of mud
turn green again?
Where do the memoirs goes as the recollections slowly fade?
And who will tend the toys in the cupboard now summer has
arrived?

The Reader

I'm such a rotten reader – the worst in all the class,
I splutter…. stutter across the page while others stifle laughs.

But teacher always promises 'that things will come in time'
So I hope Governments won't ever legislate and make my
skills a crime!

The Invitation

What's the colour of the envelope - that's wrapped around
your sigh?
Is it white, cream, or coffee - or the shade of banoffee pie?
Is it blanched, burnt, or caramelised - or tinged like
strawberry shake?
Is it whipped, walnut, fondant - or the shade of currant cake?
It doesn't really matter - what shade you are to me!
It's just my mother would like to know - before she asks you
back for tea?

A Son of Salford

You worked with Feral Ferrets and Bop Deluxe
outrage,
When Salford Son's raged anarchy – at Salford Tech
tirade,
And disguised by love of innocents – you played your
gimmicks loud,
As pistols posed and then composed – banshees rued
the crowd.
So are you an action man, a business man, a Basildon
garden Haiku?
Will bluebird scented summers swoon, like the words I
give to you?
Will health fanatics reign praises, with the lunacy of
your friends?
As emotion dregs of fables force, visit and stifle their
amends!
So what became of Lenny and his caustic coated prose?
That haunted streets of Beasley and Chicken Town
expo's,
Where cries from waking pavements kept waxing from
the stall,
Echoes of absolution resonated passively around the
Gaberdine Hall.
So goodbye Johnny Clark and give thanks to the
monotone phrase,
That gave substance to my being and brought me colour
days,
When social tides of powder stalked odes to your
profession.
I indulged my love of words and forged my own
obsession!

Lightning Source UK Ltd.
Milton Keynes UK
UKOW03f2128100214

226247UK00001B/4/P

9 781784 072858